Rookie
biographies™

Dr. Seuss

By Dana Meachen Rau

Consultant
Jeanne Clidas, Ph.D.
National Reading Consultant
and
Professor of Reading, SUNY Brockport

Children's Press ®
A Division of Scholastic Inc.
New York   Toronto   London   Auckland   Sydney
Mexico City   New Delhi   Hong Kong
Danbury, Connecticut

Designer: Herman Adler Design
Photo Researcher: Caroline Anderson
The photo on the cover shows Theodor Seuss Geisel.

Library of Congress Cataloging-in-Publication Data

Rau, Dana Meachen, 1971-
  Dr. Seuss / By Dana Meachen Rau.
    p. cm. — (Rookie biographies)
Includes index.
Summary: Presents a brief overview of the life of the man who wrote
"Green Eggs and Ham" and many other beloved children's books.
  ISBN 0-516-22593-6 (lib. bdg.)   0-516-26964-X (pbk.)
  1. Seuss, Dr.—Juvenile literature. 2. Authors, American—20th
century—Biography—Juvenile literature. 3. Illustrators—United
States—Biography—Juvenile literature. 4. Children's
literature—Authorship—Juvenile literature. [1. Seuss, Dr. 2. Authors,
American. 3. Illustrators.] I. Title: Doctor Seuss. II. Title. III.
Series: Rookie biography.
  PS3513.E2 Z8 2003
  813'.52—dc21
                                         2002015152

Have you ever heard of the Sneetches or the Grinch?

They are just a few of the funny characters (KA-rik-turs) in books by Dr. Seuss.

6

Dr. Seuss's real name was Theodor Seuss Geisel. He was born on March 2, 1904, in Springfield, Massachusetts.

His parents called him Ted. Ted had a big imagination. He liked to tell stories and draw pictures of silly animals.

When Ted grew up, he went to Dartmouth College in New Hampshire. He wrote for the school's magazine and newspaper.

After college, he drew cartoons for magazines. He changed his name to Dr. Seuss so he would seem more important.

One of his jobs was to draw cartoons of bugs for a bug spray called Flit.

11

In 1936, Dr. Seuss wrote his first book while on a ship. He wrote a story to go with the rhythm of the ship's engine. He used a lot of rhyming words. The story was called *And to Think That I Saw It on Mulberry Street.*

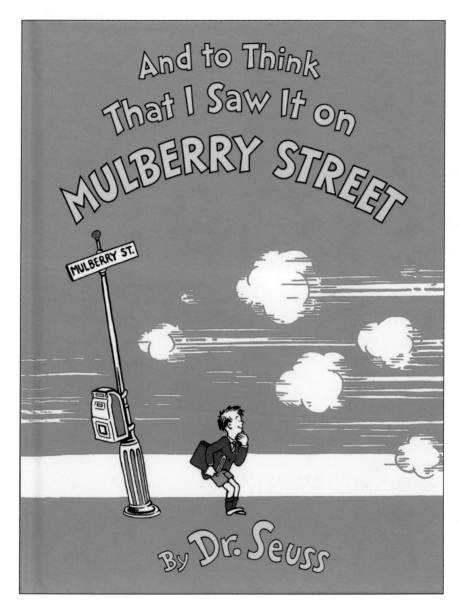

In the 1950s, some people thought many children's books were boring. They wanted better books to teach children how to read.

Dr. Seuss wrote *The Cat in the Hat*. This story changed the way people wrote books for children.

Children liked reading about the silly cat. So Dr. Seuss wrote another book. It was called *The Cat in the Hat Comes Back*. Soon there were Cat-in-the-Hat toys and lunch boxes.

A Cat-in-the-Hat balloon even floated in a parade.

Dr. Seuss wrote many more stories. One of them was *Green Eggs and Ham*. He wrote it using only fifty different words.

Dr. Seuss was never afraid to be silly. He made up words, such as "oobleck" and "Gluppity-Glupp." He also made up animals and people, such as Bar-ba-loots, tweetle beetles, and Zooks.

Dr. Seuss's books talked about important things, too. *The Lorax* is about protecting plants and animals.

23

Horton Hears a Who! is about caring for all types of people.

When Dr. Seuss grew older, he even wrote a book for adults. It was called *You're Only Old Once!* It was his last book.

Dr. Seuss died on September 24, 1991, in La Jolla, California. He was 87 years old.

Many children love books by
Dr. Seuss. His books show us
how much fun reading can be.

Which Dr. Seuss book is
your favorite?

Words You Know

Sneetches

Dr. Seuss

Springfield, Massachusetts

Dartmouth College

cartoon

The Cat in the Hat

parade

The Lorax

31

Index

About the Author

Dana Meachen Rau is the author of more than sixty books for children, including early readers, nonfiction, storybooks, and biographies. She also works as a children's book editor and illustrator. She reads Dr. Seuss stories with her husband, Chris and children, Charlie and Allison, in Farmington, Connecticut. Their favorite is *One Fish, Two Fish, Red Fish, Blue Fish*.

Photo Credits

Photographs © 2003: AP/Wide World Photos: 28 (Clint Keller/The Journal Gazette), cover, 5, 30 top right; Corbis Images: 16, 27 (Bettmann), 9, 30 bottom right (Robert Y. Kaufman/Yogi, Inc.), 23 (Joel W. Rogers); CT Valley Historical Museum: 6, 30 bottom left; Dartmouth College Library: 8; Deborah Goodsite/Swedish American Liner postcard: 12; Getty Images/Evan Agostini/Liaison: 17, 31 bottom left; Hulton|Archive/Getty Images/Gene Lester: 14, 31 top right; PhotoEdit/Don Smetzer: 19; Random House, Inc.: 22, 31 bottom right (From THE LORAX by Dr. Seuss, ® & copyright © by Dr. Seuss Enterprises, L.P. 1971, renewed 1999. Used by permission of Random House Children's Books), 13 (From AND TO THINK THAT I SAW IT ON MULBERRY STREET by Dr. Seuss, ™ & copyright © by Dr. Seuss Enterprises, L.P. 1937, renewed 1965. Used by permission of Random House Children's Books), 3, 30 top left (From THE SNEETCHES AND OTHER STORIES by Dr. Seuss, ™ & copyright © by Dr. Suess Enterprises, L.P. 1953, 1954, 1961, renewed 1989. Used by permission of Random House Children's Books); TimePix: 20 (John Bryson), 24 (Steve Liss); University of California, San Diego: 11, 31 top left (Mandeville Special Collections).